D0466125

MVFOL

IDA B. WELLS

**Discover history's heroes
and their stories.**

Michael Collins

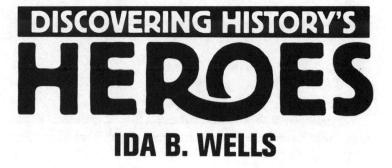

DISCOVERING HISTORY'S HEROES

IDA B. WELLS

BY DIANE BAILEY

Aladdin

New York   London   Toronto   Sydney   New Delhi

ALADDIN

An imprint of Simon & Schuster Children's Publishing Division

1230 Avenue of the Americas, New York, New York 10020

First Aladdin hardcover edition August 2019

Text copyright © 2019 by Diane Bailey

Jacket illustration copyright © 2019 by Lisa K. Weber

Also available in an Aladdin paperback edition.

All rights reserved, including the right of reproduction

in whole or in part in any form.

ALADDIN and related logo are registered trademarks of Simon & Schuster, Inc.

For information about special discounts for bulk purchases,

please contact Simon & Schuster Special Sales at

1-866-506-1949 or business@simonandschuster.com.

The Simon & Schuster Speakers Bureau can bring authors to your live

event. For more information or to book an event contact the

Simon & Schuster Speakers Bureau at 1-866-248-3049

or visit our website at www.simonspeakers.com.

Jacket designed by Nina Simoneaux

Interior designed by Mike Rosamilia

The text of this book was set in Adobe Caslon Pro.

Manufactured in the United States of America 0719 FFG

2 4 6 8 10 9 7 5 3 1

Library of Congress Control Number 2019933145

ISBN 978-1-5344-2485-2 (hc)

ISBN 978-1-5344-2484-5 (pbk)

ISBN 978-1-5344-2486-9 (eBook)

CONTENTS

IDA B. WELLS

THE TRAIN TO HOLLY SPRINGS

The train whistled as it pulled into the station, and Ida B. Wells got ready to board. The other people at the station glanced at her. They looked worried. A few spoke up. "Don't get on the train," they told her. "Don't go to Holly Springs."

The train came to a stop. No other passengers were on it. It was a freight train. There were no passenger trains running to Holly Springs, Mississippi, Ida's hometown. Right now people were desperately trying to get *away* from the town. Everyone except

Ida. She was determined to go home—no matter what anyone said.

Ida had gotten terrible news a few days before. It was 1878, and a disease called yellow fever had invaded Holly Springs. Hundreds of people had caught the illness and died. Ida's parents had been among the victims. Now she and her younger siblings were orphans. However, the **epidemic** wasn't over. If Ida went home, she might get sick and die too. But what choice did she have? She was the oldest. With her parents gone, Ida had to take care of her family.

The townspeople shook their heads, but they could not stop Ida from doing what she wanted. Clutching her bag, she stepped onto the train. What would she find when she got home?

Look! The conductor frowned and pointed at the train's caboose, where a black cloth hung. The cloth was there to honor two of the train's conductors who had recently died from yellow fever. Black was the color of death and mourning. The conductor told her the same thing the people at the station had said. She was making a big mistake by going to Holly Springs.

Ida stood her ground. She had a question for the conductor. If Holly Springs was so dangerous, why was *he* going there? He shrugged. Running the train was his job, he said. Someone had to do it.

"That's exactly why I am going home," Ida shot back. "I am the oldest of seven living children. There's nobody but me to look after them now."[1]

Ida was only sixteen years old. She didn't know how she would manage, but she knew she had no choice. She was strong. She was devoted to her family. She would find a way.

Ida B. Wells was a young African American woman. She learned early in life what she needed to do, and she was never afraid to do it. It didn't matter if it was a lot of hard work. It didn't matter if it was dangerous. It didn't matter if it meant standing up against powerful or hateful people. Ida was never a person who backed down from a fight. She even took on the subject of lynching, writing and lecturing about it, and in 1898 she was one of those protesting in Washington, DC, and calling for President William McKinley to make reforms.

In the late 1800s and early 1900s, African Americans struggled hard to be treated equally to whites. Ida became one of the first leaders in this fight for **civil rights**. Thanks to her, millions of African Americans have led better lives.

1.
GROWING UP FREE

July 16, 1862, started like any other day in Holly
Springs, Mississippi. People got up to eat breakfast,
got dressed, and went to work. That was what usually happened in the Wells family too. But on this
summer day, Lizzie Wells put a hand on her large
stomach and looked over at her husband, Jim. Today
would be different for them.

"Waaahhhhh!" Not long after, a baby's cry cut
through the air, and Jim and Lizzie welcomed their
first child into the world. They named her Ida Bell.

Ida took a deep breath. "Waaahhhh!" She let out another cry, just in case anyone had missed it the first time. She made sure everyone knew she had arrived. It was the first time she made herself heard, but it would not be the last.

The Wellses were African American, and they were slaves. Because her parents were slaves, Ida automatically became a slave when she was born. In Mississippi and several other states in the South, most black people were slaves. Slaves had no rights as people. They were treated like property. They could be sold, just like a house or an animal, and they worked for their white owners for no pay.

Most of them labored in the fields on large farms called plantations. From dawn to dusk they tended the crops. Children did not go to school. Instead they started working as soon as they were old enough. When children got to be around six years old, they carried water to the adults in the fields. By the time they turned eight or nine, they went to work in the fields themselves.

Some slaves led slightly better lives. Ida's parents were among the lucky ones. They were owned by Spires Boling, a white man who was an architect. Jim and Lizzie Wells didn't have to work in the fields. They had other skills. Jim was a carpenter, so he built things for Boling, while Lizzie worked as a cook. Unlike many slave owners, who beat their slaves and gave them very little to eat, Boling treated his slaves fairly well.

But that did not make them free.

Ida was born during a time when the United States was undergoing big changes. The Civil War had started in 1861, the year before her birth. The war was primarily about slavery. People in the country's Southern states believed white people should be able to own slaves. People in the Northern states thought that slaves should be free, just like other Americans. The country split apart over the issue.

For four years the North and the South battled

each other. At times the North seemed to be winning. At other times the South surged ahead. Like other Americans the Wellses followed news of the war closely. If the North won, slaves would be freed. Should they get their hopes up?

Ida was about to turn three years old when the war finally ended in 1865. The Northern states had won, and the slaves were set free. It was an exciting time for the Wells family. Finally they could choose what to do with their lives.

At first Ida's father stayed with Spires Boling. Jim Wells continued to work as a carpenter, but now he earned money. Then Jim had a disagreement with his employer. Before the war, slaves had not been allowed to vote. Now that black people were free, they had more rights. Some African Americans could even vote—and Jim Wells was one of them. He got his first chance during an 1867 election in Holly Springs. Jim's boss, Boling, wanted a certain man to win, and told Jim to vote for him. Jim had other ideas. He did not like Boling's choice, and voted for someone else. When Boling found out what Jim had done, he decided to punish the Wells family. Jim got home from voting to find that he had been locked out of his carpentry shop. He was out of a job. Fortunately, the family had saved some money. They rented a different house across the street, and Jim started his own business.

Ida was just five years old when this happened, but it taught her an important lesson. Her father was a man who stood up for himself and his beliefs.

The Wells family was growing. After Ida was born, her parents had three more daughters, Eugenia, Annie, and Lily. They also had four sons. Their names were James, George, Stanley, and Eddie. (Eddie died when he was a baby.)

The Wellses were a strict but happy family. They went to church each Sunday, and Ida grew up with a strong faith in God. Her parents taught their children good manners. Ida always called adults "Mr." and "Mrs." She stood up when an adult came into the room, and waited for the older person to take a seat. And she knew how to act like a lady. For example, she would never be caught eating food on the street. Only girls who had not been raised right would do that.

In a big family there were always chores to do. Ida helped her mother cook and keep house. She also looked after her younger siblings. Each Saturday night she made sure her brothers and sisters were ready for church the next morning. She helped them take their baths. She laid out their clothes. She checked to see that their shoes were polished.

Because black people were free, the Wells children were allowed to go to school. Years later Ida wrote an **autobiography**. In it she remembered that her parents had told their children that they had one main job. It was "to go to school and learn all we could."[2]

Ida loved being in the classroom. She especially

loved books. She read the Bible and all of the plays by the famous writer William Shakespeare. She liked *Little Women* by Louisa May Alcott and *A Christmas Carol* by Charles Dickens. She read the adventure stories of Oliver Optic's books for boys. It did not matter that she was not a boy. A good story was still a good story!

For a little while Ida's mother went to school with her. She wanted to learn to read so that she could study the Bible. Ida's father never learned how, but that was okay. Ida was happy to read the newspaper to him. That way she learned what was happening in the world.

Ida knew that life could be very hard for African Americans. They were not slaves anymore, but they still faced a lot of **prejudice**, especially in the South. Many white people didn't want black people to have rights, like being able to own property or vote. Daily living was also unfair for black people. Children went to **segregated** schools, so that white and black students were not mixed in the same building. Blacks had to use separate bathrooms. They could not eat at "whites only" restaurants or sleep at "whites only" hotels. If a black person and a white person met on the sidewalk, the black person always had to step aside and let the white person go first.

This was the country Ida grew up in. But she also came from a strong, happy family. She was getting an education. She was luckier than many other African Americans.

Then, when she turned sixteen, everything changed.

2.
HEAD OF
THE CLASS

In the summer of 1878, Ida packed her bags. She was getting ready to take a trip. Her grandmother, Peggy, lived a few miles from Holly Springs. It was time to harvest cotton, and Ida was a good worker. She would be a big help to her grandmother.

While Ida was gone, yellow fever arrived in the city of Memphis, Tennessee. Memphis was only about fifty miles from Holly Springs. Still, the people in Holly Springs weren't worried. People thought yellow fever came from the air in swamps, which were found on low ground. Holly Springs was on high ground, so everyone thought it would be safe. In fact, a lot of people traveled to Holly Springs to escape Memphis. They were going to wait there until the fever died down.

Unfortunately, it turned out that the town was not safe. Today we know that yellow fever spreads through mosquito bites. Even places on high ground will be dangerous if there are mosquitoes—and there were plenty of mosquitoes in Holly Springs. Soon people began getting sick. Ida's parents were busy trying to help. They were not able to leave Holly Springs, and they caught the disease too. Ida's mother got sick first, and then her father.

Ida was still at her grandmother's farm. She had no idea what was happening. Then, one day, some friends of her parents showed up. Ida invited them into the house. When she asked how everyone was doing at home, one of the men handed her a letter. She opened it and read the awful news. "Jim and

Lizzie Wells have both died of the fever," the letter said. "They died within twenty-four hours of each other. The children are all at home. . . . Send word to Ida."[3]

Grandmother Peggy and her husband thought it was too dangerous for Ida to go home. Ida disagreed. She packed her things and went to the train station. The townspeople and the train conductor told her to stay away from the infected town, but Ida didn't listen. She was determined to go home.

When Ida arrived home, she got another shock. In the past few days, her little brother Stanley had also died from yellow fever. Friends of the Wells family wanted to help the orphaned children. They held a meeting to decide what to do.

Ida was just a sixteen-year-old girl, so the adults didn't ask her what she thought. But she listened closely as they talked. They made a plan for her two brothers, James and George. James was twelve years old, and George was eight. Both of them could go to families where they could learn to be carpenters. Other families would take her sisters Annie and Lily, who were five and two. Another sister, fifteen-year-old Eugenia, was disabled. No one wanted to take her. She would have to go to a poorhouse. And Ida? The adults didn't worry about her. They thought she was old enough to take care of herself.

Ida couldn't believe what she was hearing. If she was old enough to take care of herself, then she was old enough to have a say in her own family! Ida hated the idea of splitting up her sisters and brothers. "[You are] not going to put any of the children anywhere," she said.[4] The adults looked at her in surprise, but Ida held firm. She offered them a deal: if they would help her find work, she would take care of her brothers and sisters.

Ida's hard work in school was about to pay off. In the rural areas of Mississippi that surrounded Holly Springs, it was difficult to find good teachers.

Teachers worked hard, and they did not make much money. Ida didn't care. She needed to make a living. Teaching was her best chance. If she could pass a test, she could get a job. Her parents had left behind three hundred dollars. For the next few months the family lived off their savings while Ida studied. She had to pass that test!

Luckily, she did. She was hired to teach at a school for black children. It had only one room. Children of all ages learned together. Ida was used to being in charge of her little siblings. Now she would be responsible for other people's children. She decided she had better look like an adult. Ida was short (probably about five feet), and she couldn't make herself any taller. But she *could* take out the hem of her skirt and make her dress longer. That made her look more mature.

The school was about six miles from her home. To get there Ida rode her mule, Ginger. Mules are known to be slow and stubborn, and Ginger was no different. Ida got frustrated with her. It didn't matter how many times she yelled, "Giddyap!" Ginger always plodded along at the same, slow pace.

The school was too far away for Ida to travel back and forth every day. Instead she rode there each Sunday evening. During the week she stayed with the families of her students. On Friday afternoons she climbed back onto Ginger and rode home. Grandmother Peggy moved to Holly Springs to take care of the younger children during the week.

Ida made twenty-five dollars a month. It was not a lot, but her students helped out. They brought butter and eggs for her to take home on the weekend. When she put these things together with the money she earned, Ida could support her family.

Ida was a hard worker. She spent her whole week teaching. On the weekends she went home to wash and iron clothes, cook meals, and grade papers. During the summer she took a break from teaching. She went back to being a student. She took classes at Shaw University, which was in Holly Springs. She was working to get a college degree. That would help her get a better job. Ida was strong, but her life was work, work, work, all the time. After a few years she was tired!

In 1881 one of Ida's aunts, Fannie, came to the rescue. She suggested that Ida and her sisters come to live with her in Memphis. By now James and George were living with other families. They were training to be carpenters, like their father. Fannie had lost her husband to yellow fever a few years before. If the girls moved in with her, they could help Fannie with her young children. Ida could get another job, and her salary would help pay the rent. It certainly would be an easier life. Ida accepted, and she, Annie, and Lily moved in with Fannie. (Eugenia went to live with another relative, Aunt Belle.)

Ida got a new teaching job about ten miles north of Memphis where she made thirty dollars a month. Now she took the train to work. That was a lot better than kicking that old mule, Ginger! But Ida soon found out that riding the train brought a different kind of trouble.

3.
KICKED OFF
A TRAIN

One day in September 1883, a train rumbled along the tracks. It was headed north out of Memphis. Ida was on the train, on her way to teach school. She had her bag with her. She wore gloves and a hat and carried an umbrella. She also wore a light overcoat called a duster. It would protect her clothes, since traveling could be dirty business. Ida always cared about how she looked. She bought the best clothes she could afford. She wanted people to see her as a respectable lady, and one way to do that was to dress well. She took a seat in the ladies' section, where she settled in to read a newspaper during the short journey. Ida didn't know that her careful, ladylike behavior was about to be tested.

After a few minutes the conductor came over. Ida handed him her ticket, but he refused to take it. Instead he told her she had to move to the "colored" car. (At the time, "colored" was acceptable as a word to describe black people.) Ida looked at him in surprise. She had ridden in the ladies' car many times before. No one had ever asked her to leave.

"No," she told the conductor. She did not intend to move, no matter what he said. The other car, in addition to being for black passengers, was known as the "smokers' car." White men who wanted to smoke, drink alcohol, and use bad language also rode in that car. Ida wanted none of that! It was no place for a lady. She refused to move.

The conductor insisted. He took her umbrella and bag to the other car, hoping she would follow. Ida stayed put. Then the conductor became angry. He took her arm and tried to pull her out of her seat. Ida was angry too. She fought back. She even bit the conductor's hand! He let go then!

That was not the end of it. The conductor got help from two other white men. All three of them grabbed Ida and tried to drag her off the train. Ida planted her feet on the seat in front of her and tugged back. The struggle was making a huge scene. Several white people gathered to watch and cheer the men on.

Ida fought hard, but it was one woman against three men. After a few minutes the men over-powered her. Still, Ida refused to go to the "colored" coach. Instead she got off the train at the next station. Her pride was hurt and her duster was ripped. Otherwise, though, she was all right. She even still had her train ticket.

It was not the only time Ida had trouble when she tried to ride the train. A few months later, in May 1884, she had another run-in with railroad employees who would not let her into the ladies' car because she was black. Once again, she got off the train.

Ida knew that how the railroad men had acted was wrong, and she decided to fight back. She filed a **lawsuit** against the railroad company. She wanted to prove that **discrimination** had been used against her. Ida hired a lawyer. He was black too, so Ida believed he would want to help her. Unfortunately, her lawyer was more interested in money than in justice. Ida later found out that the railroad was paying him to lose the case on purpose. Ida was disappointed, but she didn't give up. She hired another lawyer. This one was white, but he was committed to the idea of fairness. He argued the case well and won. The court said the railroad company was wrong. It ordered the railroad to pay five hundred dollars to Ida.

As it happened, it was only the first round of a bigger fight. The railroad decided to **appeal** the court's decision. The company went back to court and complained that the decision against the railroad had been wrong. They argued for the case to be tried again. This process went on for several more years, until 1887. In the end the decision was reversed, and Ida lost. She would not get her five hundred dollars. Instead the court ruled that she owed more than two hundred dollars to pay for expenses. "I had hoped [for] such great things," Ida wrote in her diary. "I have firmly believed all along that the law was on our side and would . . . give us justice. I feel . . . utterly discouraged."[5]

Ida had lost the court case, but she had taken an important stand. In the years to come, other African Americans would also refuse to give up their seats on trains and buses. Sometimes they would get kicked off. Sometimes they would get arrested. But one by one they would fight back. Eventually they would win the right to sit wherever they wanted.

Long before her court case was decided, Ida's life changed so that she didn't have to take the train to work. She had been studying hard and had passed the test to be a teacher within the city of Memphis, closer to where she lived. This test had been harder than the one for teaching in a rural school—but that meant she could get a better-paying job.

In the fall of 1884 she began teaching first grade in the city. Now she didn't need to travel very far. Plus, she got a raise to fifty dollars a month. That was about twenty dollars a month more than she had been making. Ida worked hard for that money. Every day she had to manage a classroom of forty-eight students. Sometimes she had to work to keep her temper!

She did her best to be a good teacher. But each evening and on the weekends, she tried to forget about her job. She lived in a big city now. She wanted to take advantage of everything Memphis had to offer.

4.
LIFE IN MEMPHIS

A few days after Christmas in 1885, Ida sat down and started to write. It was the beginning of a diary she kept for the next two years. She wrote about all the things that happened in her life, big and small. Today it's known as Ida's "Memphis diary" because that's where she was living at the time. However, she was on a trip home to Holly Springs when she wrote the very first entry. By now she was used to Memphis, and Holly Springs felt unfamiliar. "How strange everything seems!" Ida observed in her diary.[6]

Life in Memphis was very different from life in her hometown. Holly Springs was a small town snuggled in among farms. Memphis was right on the Mississippi River. It had thirty-five thousand people—approximately ten times as many as Holly Springs. In Memphis people drove carriages on streets paved with cobblestones. There were theaters and department stores. All day long the shouts of workers on steamboats and cotton **barges** floated across the Mississippi River. In Memphis there was always something going on.

Ida had come to Memphis with her sisters to live with Aunt Fannie. Then Fannie decided to move to California. She took Annie and Lily with her. Ida stayed in Memphis, but she couldn't live in Fannie's house anymore. She had to find rooms to rent, and they cost ten to fifteen dollars a month. That was a big chunk of her paycheck.

Ida struggled to pay her bills. She had her own

expenses, and she gave money to Fannie every month to help pay for things for her sisters. She also sent money to her brothers and to her sister Eugenia. On top of all that, Ida wasn't very good at managing her money. If she made a budget, she didn't stick to it! Instead she bought the things she wanted. She especially liked clothes. When she saw a pretty dress or hat, she could not pass it up. These bad habits caught up with her. Several times she didn't have enough money to pay her rent. The landlords made her leave, and she had to find a new place to live.

Even though she was always short on money, Ida enjoyed living in Memphis. In many places in the South, most black people were poor. They often did the same kind of work they had done as slaves. A lot were **sharecroppers**, doing farmwork for white bosses who kept most of the money. But Memphis had a strong community of middle-class blacks who worked as policemen, mailmen, barbers, and blacksmiths. Ida made friends with them and their families.

Without her sisters to look after, Ida also had time for a social life. Almost every day brought something new. She went to parties on Friday nights and church on Sunday mornings. She went horseback riding (and fell off the horse). She attended her first professional baseball game (and lost her temper when a Memphis player made an error and the team lost). On the days when she stayed home, she took care of chores like washing and ironing her clothes. Sometimes she felt lazy. One day she reported in her diary, "The biggest job undertaken and finished was—a bath."[7]

When she went on a date, Ida was able to see plays and concerts. Sometimes her date took her to a dance. They took walks and played checkers. At the time it was unusual for young, single women to go out in public alone. Having a man to **escort** her made it easier for Ida to enjoy these activities. In the late 1800s most women got married by the time they were in their early twenties. Ida was different.

She liked having male friends, but she didn't want to marry any of them!

Ida had spent her childhood doing the things that wives and mothers did. Now she wanted to do something else. But what was it? At one point she wrote in her diary, "I wonder what kind of a creature I will eventually become?"[8]

In the summer of 1886, Ida traveled to California to visit her sisters and Aunt Fannie. Fannie wanted Ida to move out and live with them. Ida thought about it and decided to give it a try. She liked Memphis, but it would be nice to be closer to her family. She found a teaching job in California, but after only one day she knew she'd made a mistake. She hated the new job. She quit on the second day and made plans to move to the Midwest. Her sister Annie stayed with Aunt Fannie, but Lily returned with Ida.

Ida had another job offer in Kansas City, Missouri. That job didn't last long either. Ida found out that the school had had too many teachers. They had fired another teacher to make room for her. The other teachers resented her for it. Once again Ida quit. This time she went back to Memphis. She started teaching again there. In only two weeks Ida had taught in three different states!

Traveling all over the country, Ida had seen how blacks lived in different cities. One thing was the same everywhere: blacks didn't have the same rights as whites. They were treated like second-class citizens. It was worst in the South. A growing problem was **lynching**. A person would be accused of a crime. Sometimes the person had committed the crime, and sometimes not. Often the truth didn't matter. The accused person would be attacked by a mob of people and killed. The mob would say that they were getting "justice." It was uncommon for a white person or a woman to be lynched. Most victims were black men.

Most lynchings happened in the Southern states, where **racism** was a big problem. But no one did much to stop them. Ida thought lynching was horrifying. She could not accept this terrible practice, and she made it her life's work to stop it.

Ida's Memphis diary tells a lot about her life as a young woman. It also shows Ida developing her talent for writing. At first she wrote just for herself. That would change. Before long she would bring her words to thousands of people.

5.
PRINCESS OF
THE PRESS

Perhaps I was rash
But he's after my cash!
I see through his plans like a book.[9]

Ida hadn't written those particular lines, but she knew what people liked. The audience laughed as Ida recited the funny poem. "The Widow Bud" was about a woman who rejects all the men who are interested in her. The silly rhymes were always popular with the audience.

Ida liked to perform. She even thought about being an actress, and took speech lessons to improve her speaking. The lessons cost fifty cents apiece. That was a lot of money, but Ida thought it was worth it. Whenever she could scrape together the money, she spent Saturday mornings with her teacher, who gave her different assignments. Ida practiced at home and then performed in public. On Friday evenings she went to meetings of a type of literary club called a **lyceum**. The members always had a good time reading poems and essays out loud. They put on skits and played music.

The lyceum had a serious side too. Most of the members were teachers, like Ida. They talked about politics and other issues. The group also had its own newsletter, the *Evening Star*. It had poems, book reviews, and bits of news. At the end of each meeting, the editor of the *Star* read it to the group. When the editor moved out of town, the members asked Ida to take over. Ida loved putting the newsletter together and reading it out loud, and everyone thought she did a good job. Those speech lessons were paying off! When it came to writing and reading the *Star*, Ida *was* a "star." Word spread, and people from outside the group started to come to the meetings. They wanted to hear her too.

The Reverend R. N. Countee was a minister at a Memphis church. He also published a newspaper called the *Living Way*. One night he came to listen to Ida speak. He liked what he heard, and he asked Ida if she would like to write a weekly column for the *Living Way*. Yes, she would! Ida jumped at the chance. In the *Living Way* she could write about important subjects. Ida thought she would like a career as a **journalist**. This could be her start.

Ida decided to use a pen name, "Iola." A pen name is not a writer's real name. It's a name they make up to use on their stories or articles. Writers don't use pen names all the time, but sometimes they like to "be" someone else when they are writing.

Years later Ida's daughter would explain where "Iola" had come from. One time, Ida had seen her name written down. Whoever had written it had used sloppy handwriting. The parts of the letter *d* didn't connect. The *d* actually looked like an *o* and an *l*. Instead of "Ida," it looked like "Iola." Ida decided she liked it, though, and took it as her pen name.

Ida wasn't sure she had enough skill to be a writer. She didn't think she had any talent in that department. In truth Ida was a powerful writer. She was clear and direct. She tried not to use big words when simple ones would work fine. And she wasn't afraid to give her opinion. "It may be unwise to express myself so strongly but I cannot help it," she wrote in her diary.[10]

In the 1880s the **press** was made up mostly of white men. Women journalists were uncommon. Black women were even more rare. However, more and more newspapers were starting up. A lot of them were aimed at African Americans. Ida was getting into the business at a good time.

Most female journalists wrote about "women's" topics. They offered advice on things like marriage, children, or running a household. Ida had nothing against marriage, children, or households. On the other hand, she didn't want to write about them. Instead she wanted to talk about the problem she saw all around her: racism. She wrote blunt articles for the *Living Way* that criticized white people for treating blacks poorly. She also blamed black people who did not defend their rights.

Reverend Countee sent the *Living Way* to other newspapers all over the country. Sometimes the editors asked Ida to write articles for their papers too. Her words were making their way to Arkansas, Indiana, Michigan, Missouri, and Washington, DC.

Ida also got to travel. At one meeting for black journalists, she was excited to meet Frederick Douglass. Douglass was a black man who had been a slave before the Civil War. He had been able to escape from slavery, and after the war he had become a leader in the black community. Now he was the most famous and important black man in the country. Ida respected his work to help African Americans get civil rights. It was exactly what she wanted to do.

She also met T. Thomas Fortune. Fortune was just a few years older than Ida. Like her, he had been born a slave. Now he edited a large newspaper called the *New York Age*. He was impressed with Ida. He wrote in his newspaper, "She has plenty of nerve . . . and she has no sympathy with humbug."[11] By that, Fortune meant Ida would not put up with any nonsense!

Ida was becoming better known. The editor of the *American Baptist* newspaper traveled to Memphis to meet Ida in person. He also wanted Ida to write for his paper. Usually Ida got free copies of a newspaper in exchange for writing an article. But the *American Baptist* editor offered something else—money! He would pay her a dollar a week. That wasn't enough to live on, but Ida was still excited. "It was the first time anyone had offered to pay me for the work I had enjoyed doing," she wrote later.[12] Ida loved her work, and her readers loved her. She even got a nickname, the Princess of the Press.

In addition to her work for the *Living Way*, in 1889 Ida began to work for another Memphis newspaper called the *Free Speech and Headlight*. She even bought part of the paper. She and two men each owned one-third of it. Ida was the most hands-on of the three of them. She changed the name of the paper to *Free Speech*, to make it shorter and snappier. Then she started writing the fiery, controversial articles that she was known for.

In 1891 Ida wrote a story that criticized the Memphis school system. She pointed out that the buildings where African Americans attended school were run-down, and argued that some of the staff hired to teach black children weren't qualified for their jobs. As a result Memphis's black children were getting a worse education than white children. The article caused an uproar. Ida was still teaching in Memphis schools at the time. School officials were so angry, they fired her.

For years Ida had wanted to work full-time as a journalist. Now, like it or not, she was getting her wish.

6.
A TERRIBLE TRAGEDY

The black man on the train waited for the newspaper salesman to come down the aisle. He knew exactly which paper he wanted to buy. The pink one! He pointed at *Free Speech* and held out his coins. He could not read, but that didn't matter. He would have a friend read it to him later.

Ida had come up with the idea of printing *Free Speech* on pink paper. It would stand out that way. Hopefully it would attract customers. Now that she earned all her money from the paper, Ida needed every reader she could get!

Ida had thrown herself into making *Free Speech* successful. She traveled all over to find people to **subscribe** to the newspaper. She had a knack for convincing people to buy her paper. She wrote that she left one meeting "weighted down with silver dollars."[13] Her very next stop was the bank! Her hard work paid off. In a few months she was selling more than twice as many copies of *Free Speech* as had been sold previously. One newspaper salesman said he'd never before seen so many African Americans who wanted to buy a newspaper.

Ida was making almost as much money as she had from teaching. Plus, people respected her. "I was handed from town to town . . . and treated like a queen," she wrote later.[14] Her dream of becoming a writer had come true.

Ida had all the qualities of a good journalist. She was curious and determined. She kept her eyes and ears open and always looked for the truth. And she knew when to listen to other people. Tommie Moss was a good friend of Ida's. He was a mailman, and the *Free Speech* office was on his route. Walking around town all day, Tommie heard lots of news, and he made sure to tell Ida so that she could put it in the paper.

One day Tommie shared his own news. He had started a new business to earn extra money. Along with two partners, he'd opened a store called the People's Grocery. The new store was in an area of town known as "the Curve," because the track for the **streetcar** curved there. Some white people lived there, but mostly it was a neighborhood of African Americans.

The People's Grocery was not the first grocery store in the area. Another one was owned by a white man named William Barrett. Before Tommie had opened his store, the people in the neighborhood had shopped at Barrett's grocery store. It had been the only one close to their homes. Now they had a choice. Many of them switched and started shopping at Tommie's store. Some of them were Tommie's friends, but it also helped that his prices were lower than Barrett's. Some white customers even came to Tommie. Barrett was angry about losing customers, however, and he didn't think it was his fault. Instead he blamed Tommie and his partners.

One day in 1892 a group of boys in the area were playing a game of marbles. Some of the boys were black, and some were white. The black boys won the game, and the white boys got upset. They all got into a fight. The fathers of the boys were nearby and saw what was happening. They got involved too. Soon the situation was out of control, with people beating one another up. By the time it was finished, everyone knew that the fight had not been about marbles at all. It had been about race.

The black men won the fight, and now William Barrett was even angrier. He accused Tommie Moss and his business partners of starting a **riot**. Barrett got a bunch of white men together into a gang. On the coming Saturday night, they were going to destroy the People's Grocery store.

Tommie quickly found out what Barrett had planned. Tommie and his partners camped out at the store so that they could defend it. At about ten o'clock that night, the white men broke in. The black storekeepers were afraid for their lives. They shot at the white men, and some of the intruders got hurt. That was enough reason for the police to arrest the black men and put them in jail.

According to the law the black men had a right to a fair trial, but Barrett's white mob didn't care about that. They wanted to see the blacks punished for standing up to whites. The whites began calling for the black men to be lynched.

Stuck in jail, Tommie and his friends were in terrible danger. They could not escape, and they could not defend themselves. For two days armed guards stood outside their cells to protect them. Everyone was waiting to find out what would happen to the white men who had gotten hurt. Would they live or die? On the third day the newspapers reported that the white men would live. That was good news. Now maybe everyone would calm down. The guards thought it was safe to leave.

They were wrong.

The next night a lynch mob came for the three black men. The mob stormed into the jail and pulled the prisoners from their cells. Then the storekeepers were put on a train and driven out of town. Tommie Moss knew what was coming. He begged for his life, saying he had a wife and children to support. The men in the mob didn't care. Minutes later the mob shot all three men to death.

Tommie had one last message for African Americans in Memphis. "Tell my people to go west," he said just before he died. "There is no justice for them here."[15]

7.
DRIVEN OUT

The news about Tommie horrified Ida. It made her sad but also very angry. She knew she could not bring her friend back, but she could help spread his message.

Tommie's last words had been "go west." There were towns that welcomed black people in places like Oklahoma, Kansas, and Colorado. Ida wrote articles in *Free Speech* urging people to leave Memphis. They took her advice. Over the next two months about six thousand blacks poured out of the city. That was about one out of every five black people living there at the time. Some took the train, while others went in wagons pulled by horses or mules. Some even walked. They were ready to go. Ida found out that many African Americans had been saving their money since even before the lynchings. They wanted to leave the racism of Memphis behind them and make a better life somewhere else.

The black people who stayed behind fought back in other ways. Many refused to work for white people. They wouldn't shop at stores owned by whites. These **boycotts** hurt white businesses. One day some men came to see Ida at the *Free Speech* office. They worked for the streetcar company, which was run by whites. The men told her that African Americans had stopped riding the streetcars. That was making the company lose money. One of the men said blacks had stopped taking the streetcars because the cars ran on electricity. He said African Americans were afraid of the new technology, and he asked Ida to write an article telling them that the streetcars were safe.

Ida gave the man a skeptical look. The streetcars had started using electric power six months before. It seemed strange that it was just now a problem. Ida asked him how long ago blacks had stopped riding the streetcars. "About six weeks," he answered.[16]

Ida did not need to look at her calendar to know what had happened six weeks before. That was when Tommie Moss and his friends had been lynched. Black people had stopped riding the streetcars in protest. Ida pointed this out, but the men argued with her. They said the people who ran the streetcar company had had nothing to do with the lynching. Ida disagreed. Whites did not have to actually be involved in the killing, she said. Plenty of them had stood by and let it happen. They were just as guilty.

Ida did end up writing an article. But it did not say what the men had wanted. Instead it told blacks to "keep up the good work" and stay off the streetcars![17]

Ida had known about lynchings before Tommie

Moss and his partners had been murdered. But he was the first person she had known personally. "This is what opened my eyes to what lynching really was," she wrote later. "[It was] an excuse to get rid of Negroes who were acquiring wealth and property."[18]

She began to look more deeply into the lynching problem. What she found troubled her. Black men were being accused of all kinds of crimes. Then white mobs claimed that they wanted to get justice for these crimes. Some lynchings were connected to actual crimes, but a lot weren't. Many were just excuses to punish people whose only "crime" was being black. Lynching was cruel and illegal, and it was getting worse. Tommie Moss was killed in 1892. More people were lynched that year than during any other year in history, before or after.

Ida published articles in *Free Speech* to **condemn** the practice. She knew this made her a target too. She even bought a gun in case she needed to protect herself. But she refused to stay silent. "I felt that one had better die fighting against injustice than to die like a dog or a rat in a trap," she wrote.[19]

Ida had been thinking about leaving Memphis too. She had already visited Oklahoma. Now she was about to take another trip. This time she would visit the Northeast. Her final stop was New York, where she would meet with her friend T. Thomas Fortune, the editor of the *New York Age*.

Before she left, Ida wrote another article about lynching for *Free Speech*. It was even more blunt and direct than her other ones. In the article Ida said white people should stop the violence against blacks. If they didn't, she predicted they would face trouble themselves. Ida sent the article to the printer. Then she packed her bags.

The article came out on May 21, 1892, while Ida was out of town. White people in Memphis were furious about what she had written. They believed she was threatening white people. An angry mob got together to teach her a lesson. They stormed the offices of *Free Speech*. Fortunately, Ida wasn't there. She could have gotten hurt or even killed. The mob destroyed the newspaper's offices and made it clear that Ida was not welcome back in Memphis.

Since Ida was traveling, she didn't know what was going on. She was surprised a few days later when she got off the train to meet Fortune. "Well, we've been a long time getting you to New York," he told her. "But now you are here I am afraid you will have to stay."[20]

What on earth was Fortune talking about? Ida had no idea, so Fortune filled her in. He handed her a newspaper that told of the violence in Memphis and at the *Free Speech* offices. "From the **rumpus** you have kicked up," Fortune told Ida, he believed her life was in danger.[21] After reading the paper, Ida agreed. She could not go back. Not now, anyway—and maybe not ever.

New York was her new home.

8.
TAKING THE STAGE

Ida took her seat on the stage and looked around in wonder. The auditorium was filled with flowers. Behind her, lights blazed out the word "Iola," her pen name. The ushers wore white silk badges that also had her name on them. People in the audience flipped through their programs, which were designed to look like miniature copies of *Free Speech*. Ida was impressed by all the little details. But the best part was that the audience was full of important women. They had come from all over the Northeast to hear her speak—*and* they had paid for it!

It was October 5, 1892, a few months after Ida had been forced to leave Memphis. Since then she had worked to draw attention to the problem of lynching. Shortly after coming to New York, she had sat down to write an article for the *New York Age*. It talked about Tommie Moss and lynchings in the South. T. Thomas Fortune had had a feeling that the article would be a hit. He'd printed ten thousand copies of that day's newspaper and sent them all over the country. He'd been right. One thousand copies had been sold in Memphis alone!

In New York the article grabbed the attention of some African American women. They invited Ida to give a speech where people would pay to get in. It would raise money for her to reprint the article in a booklet and send it to even more people. Ida eagerly accepted the offer.

Ida was not shy. She was used to saying what she

thought. She knew it often upset people, but she didn't care. In fact, she wanted to stir up trouble. If no one complained, nothing would change. But something felt different on that October night. All of a sudden the fearless Ida was gone. In her place was regular Ida—and that Ida had a bad case of stage fright! "A panic **seized** me," she remembered later. "I was afraid that I was going to make a scene and spoil [everything]."[22]

Ida went to the **podium**. *Do not cry!* she told herself. But as she talked about Tommie's murder, Ida got more and more upset.

Do not cry! Do not cry!

Her fierce scolding did no good. Ida began to cry. She couldn't help it. Tears streamed down her face. She was extremely embarrassed, but she did not stop talking. She reached behind her, and another woman handed her a handkerchief. Ida wiped her face and kept going. The story had to be told.

Afterward Ida was worried. She thought she'd

ruined everything by crying. The women would think she was weak. They wouldn't take her seriously. In fact, Ida's breakdown did just the opposite. The women were moved by her speech. They could tell she truly believed in what she was saying.

At the end of the evening the women gave Ida a gold pin. It was shaped like a pen. That was the perfect way to honor Ida's powerful words. She felt very grateful for the gift and wore it often for the next twenty years. The event also raised about four hundred fifty dollars. Ida used the money to publish a pamphlet about lynching. She chose the title *Southern Horrors: Lynch Law in All Its Phases*.

One person who read Ida's words was Frederick Douglass. He was one of Ida's heroes, and she was thrilled when Douglass sent her a letter praising her work. "Brave woman!" he wrote. "You have done your people and mine a service which can neither be weighed nor measured."[23]

After her speech in New York, Ida was invited to

other cities. She visited Providence, Rhode Island; Boston, Massachusetts; and Washington, DC. At a speech in Philadelphia, Pennsylvania, Ida met a woman named Catherine Impey, who was a social **activist** from Great Britain. She was traveling around America to learn more about the problems between black and white people. Like Ida, she wanted to fight racism. The two women hit it off. Soon their friendship would lead to an important invitation.

In February 1893 there was an awful lynching in Paris, Texas. A black man named Henry Smith was accused of killing a four-year-old white girl. He might have been guilty, but there was never solid proof. He also never got a trial in court where the facts could be stated fairly. Instead a lynch mob of ten thousand people reached him first. Although some lynchings happened in secret, Henry Smith's was planned from the beginning to be a public event. It was advertised in newspapers. People who lived in other states came to watch. Children got the day off from school. People collected souvenirs. Ida felt sickened that Henry Smith's murder had been turned into a celebration.

News about the lynching spread quickly. Outside of the South, most people agreed it was disgraceful. Even if Smith had been guilty, his brutal murder had been wrong. One newspaper editor wrote, "We turn our eyes away from it. It's awful, awful!"[24]

Henry Smith's story traveled all over the world. Thousands of miles away, in Great Britain, a woman named Isabelle Mayo heard about it. Mayo was another social activist. She wanted to help fight lynching, and the first step was to educate people. People in Great Britain needed to know what was happening in the United States. It would be best if someone with firsthand experience could come and talk about it. First Mayo thought about Frederick

Douglass, but he was too old to make the trip. She decided to ask her friend Catherine Impey for advice. Did Impey know anyone else who could talk about America's race problems? Impey knew just the person: Ida B. Wells.

9.
"YOU HAVE THE STORY"

Ida sat in the living room at Frederick Douglass's home in Washington, DC. She felt great respect for Douglass and knew she could learn a lot from him. When he had invited her to visit him and his wife, Helen, Ida had eagerly agreed. Douglass watched as the two women talked. They liked each other, and he was glad.

When the visit ended, Douglass took Ida to the train station. He thanked her for being kind to his wife. This surprised Ida. Why wouldn't she be kind?

Helen had been a friendly and generous hostess. Frederick told her that some people didn't care *how* Helen acted. To them it only mattered that Frederick was black and Helen was white. They did not approve of an **interracial** marriage. They were cold and distant to Helen.

Ida assured Douglass that she liked Helen. It made no difference what color her skin was. She certainly would not be rude. Ida had better manners than that! Frederick smiled. "I only wish everyone thought and acted as you do, my dear," he said.[25]

Soon the Douglasses invited Ida for another visit, and she was staying with them when a letter arrived for her. It was from Catherine Impey, the English woman Ida had met a few months earlier. Impey asked Ida to come to England. There Ida could speak about racism and lynchings. Impey had already talked to Isabelle Mayo about it, and Mayo would pay for Ida's trip.

Ida showed the letter to Douglass. Going to England was a great opportunity. She could reach a whole new group of people. If more people knew about lynching, there was a better chance to stop it. That was Ida's goal.

Still, she was not sure if she should say yes. Would someone else do a better job? Douglass assured Ida that she was the right choice. "You go, my child," he told her. "You are the one to go, for you have the story to tell."[26]

Ida had left Memphis almost a year before. During that time she had traveled all over the country giving speeches. Most black people already knew about the problem of lynching. Like Ida, they were outraged. But she needed to convince white people, who had the most power to change things. That job was a lot harder, and she was frustrated. She did not seem to be making very much progress.

Many Americans put up with racism, but that was not the case in England. In addition, Americans respected the British. Ida thought about this. Maybe she had to leave America to get Americans to pay attention! It seemed backward, but what if it worked? She could try. There was the invitation, right in front of her.

"It seemed like an open door in a stone wall," Ida wrote later.[27]

April 5, 1893, was a beautiful day. Ida boarded the steamship *Teutonic*. She was excited to start her trip to England. It was her first time crossing the ocean. Would she get seasick? She hoped not. She wasn't too worried, though. Another woman traveling with her was a doctor. If Ida did get sick, the doctor could give her some medicine. The first day went by with no problems. So did the second day. Ida wrote in her journal, "I don't think I am going to need [the doctor]." She wrote those words a little too soon. On the third day, Ida reported in her journal, "Seasick." On the fourth day she was "seasick still." The fifth day?

"Seasicker." And the sixth, "Seasickest."[28] Fortunately, she felt a little better on the seventh day. And on the ninth day the ship docked in England. Ida must have sighed with relief. Finally she could step back onto dry land!

For the most part Ida liked England. One thing tested her patience, though. The train cars were small and narrow. The seats did not all point forward, like in the United States. Instead they were arranged in sets, so that they faced each other. Whenever she rode the train, Ida spent the trip staring at the person sitting across from her, while their knees bumped. She hated that!

On the other hand, Ida could sit anywhere on the train she wanted. There were no "white" and "colored" cars. That was a nice change from the United States.

Catherine Impey and Isabelle Mayo were Ida's hostesses. The three of them worked hard to arrange speeches and set up meetings with journalists. It was a busy few months. At one event Ida was just an attendee, but the man who was scheduled to speak couldn't come. The organizers asked if Ida would step in. They told her that she could speak for fifteen minutes.

At the podium Ida described what life was like for black people in America. She talked about how black people were pressured not to vote. She talked about how black and white people got harassed if they married each other. And she talked about the violence of lynchings. The fifteen hundred people in the audience listened closely. Ida's fifteen minutes came and went. No one interrupted. What Ida was saying was too important.

Unfortunately, Ida's trip to England ended abruptly. Catherine Impey and Isabelle Mayo had a bad fight. Ida got sucked into the middle of it. One evening Mayo came to Ida and demanded that she take her side. But Ida was good friends with Impey. Ida didn't want to turn against her.

Ida stayed awake all night wondering what to do. By the morning, she had decided. She told Mayo that she would not turn her back on her friend. Mayo was furious. She refused to give Ida any more money. Ida didn't have enough money of her own to stay in England, so she was forced to return to the United States.

She was disappointed, but by the time she got home, she was ready to get back to work. As soon as her ship arrived in New York, she got on a train. She was headed straight to Chicago. She had another project waiting for her there.

10.
THE WORLD'S FAIR

Christopher Columbus arrived in America in 1492. Imagine what the land looked like then. There were no crowded cities or tall buildings. There were no cars or trains. There were no telephones or electricity.

Four hundred years later it was a very different place! Railroad tracks crossed the country from the Atlantic Ocean all the way to the Pacific. Electric lightbulbs lit up the night. Workers at factories made shirts and shoes, nails and knives, and clocks and bicycles. Americans were proud of their country. They believed it was a land of progress.

To celebrate, there was a huge World's Fair in Chicago. It had exhibits about science, art, and culture. The fair was supposed to be held in 1892, but there was too much work to finish on time. It took until 1893 to get everything ready.

The fair ran for six months, with about 150,000 people visiting each day. They gazed up at tall buildings and looked down from the top of the first Ferris wheel. They saw some of the first automobiles. They watched the flickering pictures in a movie theater.

Forty-six different countries had exhibits at the fair. People could learn about cultures from all over the world. But one culture was missing. There was almost nothing at the fair to show what African Americans had done over the years. Ida B. Wells wasn't happy about that!

Ida got to Chicago in the summer of 1893. There she met with Frederick Douglass and another man,

Ferdinand Barnett. Barnett was a lawyer in Chicago. He also published a newspaper for black people called the *Conservator*.

The three of them talked about that the fair was leaving black people out. They agreed it was unjust, but what should they do about it? Ida knew what she could do—protest! That was always a good way to make sure her voice was heard. She, Douglass, and Barnett wrote a pamphlet that they handed out at the fair. (They called it a pamphlet, but it was eighty-one pages long!) The pamphlet talked about the accomplishments of African Americans. Blacks had helped society in science, business, music, and art. The pamphlet also asked a question. Why were African Americans not part of the fair? The reason, Ida wrote, was racism.

At first the white people who'd organized the fair didn't think it was important to include African Americans, but as more and more blacks protested about being left out, the organizers changed their minds. They asked Frederick Douglass to organize a

"Colored People's Day" at the fair. It would focus on black people.

Ida hated this idea. She thought it was too little, too late. She told Douglass not to do it, but he didn't agree. He said yes to the offer. Ida was disgusted. She felt like Douglass didn't care if African Americans got treated with respect. But Douglass was older than Ida and had a lot more experience. He believed that something good could come from the day.

Still, Ida felt insulted by the whole thing. She didn't help Douglass plan the events for Colored People's Day. When the day came, she made a point to *not* go.

The next day, she read about the event in the newspaper. Douglass had done a wonderful job, and many black people had attended and heard him speak. Ida saw now that she had been wrong. She went to Douglass and apologized.

During the fair a group of African American men formed a club. They hosted visitors who came to the fair. They invited Ida to organize and speak at a special "Ladies' Day." It was very popular with the women who came. In fact, they decided to form their own club in September 1893. They named it for Ida and elected her the president. The goal of the Ida B. Wells Club was to promote civil rights. The club would bring together people who wanted to do good work in Chicago.

Ida wanted to use her influence outside of Chicago too. In early 1894 she was invited back to England. This trip went better than the first one. (For one thing, she wasn't seasick on the way over!) After she reached England, she gave more than a hundred speeches about lynching and racism in America. She impressed the people she spoke with, and many of them joined her cause.

Ida felt like people in England believed in her more than people in the United States did. At one point she wondered if she should even go back to America. She wrote to Helen Douglass (Frederick's wife) about her plans to return home. Then she added, "Home, did I say? I forgot that I have no home."[29]

It is not surprising that Ida felt that way. She had been forced to leave Memphis in 1892. For the next two years she had bounced around. First it was New York. Then it was Chicago. Twice she'd gone to England. Where was home?

However, there is a saying: "Home is where the heart is."

Ida decided her heart was in Chicago. Lots of African Americans lived in the Midwest's largest city, and more were moving there all the time. Ida felt comfortable in Chicago. Plus, she had made one very special friend—Ferdinand Barnett. Ida had fallen in love.

Ida had dated several men over the years, but she'd never found anyone she wanted to marry. That changed with Ferdinand. They had worked closely together while they'd been writing the pamphlet for the World's Fair. Ida had also begun writing for his newspaper. They got to know each other very well, and learned that they had a lot in common. Like Ida, Ferdinand cared about civil rights for African Americans, and he believed in rights for women. Ferdinand didn't care about having a traditional marriage. He knew Ida would not want to stay home, where she would only keep house and raise children. She wanted to keep working, and that was what Ferdinand wanted her to do. They were perfect for each other.

When Ferdinand asked Ida to marry him, she agreed that it was a good idea. But there was a problem. When would she find the time? Ida couldn't think about getting married yet. She had things to do first!

11.
STAYING BUSY

A man in the audience interrupted Ida. *Again*. He challenged her on everything she said. She took a deep breath. There was no use in snapping at him. She was on the road, giving speeches all over the United States. Sometimes people clapped, and sometimes they booed. She was used to this. It was just part of the job.

She went on with her speech. Soon the man shouted out another question. Did she think all lynching victims were innocent? Ida didn't believe that, but that was not the point. The point was that blacks and whites weren't treated equally, especially in the South. Ida tried patiently to answer the man's questions, but he wouldn't accept her answers. He got ruder and ruder. Finally he asked, "If Negroes are so badly treated in the South, why do they not come north or go west?"

Now a white woman jumped up. She answered the question for Ida. "Because they are treated no better in the North than they are in the South!" she exclaimed.[30]

Ida was impressed. Here was a white woman who understood what Ida was talking about. And she had stuck up for Ida! After the meeting Ida learned that the woman was Susan B. Anthony, a famous activist. She was working to get American women the right to vote.

Anthony and Ida went on to become friends. They focused on different causes. Anthony cared about voting. Ida cared about equality for blacks. But they both wanted civil rights for all Americans. They did not always agree on the best way to get what they wanted, but they respected each other.

As Ida got better known, she made more friends like Anthony. But she also made enemies. Some people accused her of just wanting attention. Some thought she was trying to make money. The *New York Times* called her "nasty-minded." The *Memphis Commercial* viciously attacked her character and said that her opinions were "foul." Even some black people were against her. J. Thomas Turner was a black journalist from Memphis. Years before, he had been a friend of Ida's. Now he turned against her. "All informed colored people know [her] statements . . . are false," he said.[31] Ida felt bad when she read these attacks, but she knew that speaking up was more important than her own feelings.

"Threats cannot **suppress** the truth."[32] Ida wrote those words in her newest book, *A Red Record*. From 1892 to 1894 hundreds of black people were lynched.

Ida had kept track of all of them. *A Red Record* listed every lynching in the United States for those three years. Ida described how the victims had been killed. She even published pictures from the scenes. They were awful to look at, but Ida wanted to get people's attention.

She also listed the crimes that the victims had been accused of. Some of the crimes were serious, such as murder. Lynching victims had also been accused of stealing and burning down buildings. Other offenses were minor. One was talking saucy to a white person. Ida could imagine what "saucy" meant. Maybe a man had said, "You look pretty in that dress, ma'am." Or maybe it had been, "I don't think that's right, sir." It didn't matter if the black person meant no harm. It only mattered what the white person thought.

White people sometimes defended lynchings. They said the punishments were justified for the crimes. Ida didn't believe that. Almost all lynchings happened to black people. They were a way for white people to keep blacks "in their place." That "place," of course, was beneath white people. Ida hoped that *A Red Record* would help show what was really happening.

Sometimes Ida's work discouraged her. As she traveled around the country giving speeches, she had to put up with cruel comments. It was almost worse when only a few people showed up to listen. At every stop, though, something brightened her day. Ferdinand Barnett missed her. He sent a letter to each city where Ida visited. The letters were waiting for her when she arrived. Back in Chicago, Ferdinand was waiting too. Waiting for Ida to come home.

By the summer of 1895, Ida was ready to start the next chapter of her life. Ferdinand had been courting her for two years. He'd asked her to marry him three different times. Finally she said yes.

Ida was very popular in Chicago. She had many

friends in the Ida B. Wells Club. They wanted to be part of the wedding. Ida didn't know how to choose among them. In the end she sent word to her sisters in California. Annie and Lily could travel to Chicago and be her bridesmaids. It was expensive, but Ida thought it was worth it. This way she wouldn't offend any of her friends!

Ferdinand and Ida picked June 27, 1895, as their wedding day. On that Thursday evening the church was crammed with people. More curious people gathered outside. It seemed like most of the city wanted to be part of the fun. Newspapers carried stories about the event. The *New York Times* had criticized Ida in the past, but its editors also knew she was famous. The paper put news of her wedding on the front page.

At the time, almost all married women gave up their maiden names (the last name they were born with). They took the last names of their husbands. But Ida didn't want to stop using the name "Wells."

By now she didn't use the name "Iola" anymore. When she wrote an article or gave a speech, she used her real name. She was building a career as Ida B. Wells.

On the other hand, she didn't want to ignore the name "Barnett." She loved Ferdinand and wanted to honor him. In the end she decided to have it both ways. She linked both names together into one. Now she was known as Ida B. Wells-Barnett.

12.
STARTING A FAMILY

Ferdinand had been married once before. He had had two sons with his first wife before she died. Now Ida had two stepsons. Ferdinand III was ten years old, and his brother, Albert, was eight. Two young boys have a lot of energy. Weren't they enough for one family? Many of the couple's friends and family thought so. Besides, the newlyweds were too old to start another family. Ida was almost thirty-three years old. Ferdinand was ten years older! That didn't matter to them. They wanted more children.

In March 1896, Ida gave birth to her first son, Charles.

Newborn babies are hard work. They cry a lot. They stay awake when everyone else wants to sleep. Ida still wanted to travel and give speeches, but she didn't see a way to do that. Charles was too young to stay home with a babysitter, because Ida still needed to nurse him. She could not take him with her either. Who would look after him while she was speaking? The people who wanted Ida to come and speak had an idea. At each town there would be a woman to take care of Charles while Ida spoke. Ida wouldn't have to worry about him.

In one town the babysitter also wanted to hear Ida's speech. She asked if she could bring baby Charles with her. Ida agreed. It turned out to be a bad plan! Charles heard his mother's voice and started to cry. It was hard for people to hear what Ida was saying. It was even harder for Ida to ignore her crying son. Another woman saw the problem and stepped in. She plucked Charles out of the babysitter's arms and took him outside. Now the babysitter could hear Ida's speech—and so could everyone else!

Charles was good at getting people's attention. In July 1896 there was a meeting of black women who were forming a new group to fight for civil rights. Of course Ida wanted to go. She took Charles with her. He was just four months old, the youngest person there. The oldest person was seventy-five years old. Her name was Harriet Tubman, and she was the most famous black woman alive. Tubman had been born a slave but had escaped in 1849. Then she had helped other slaves escape to freedom.

Someone suggested that Charles be named the "baby" of the new group. Everyone liked that idea. Tubman took Charles in her arms. Then she lifted him high over her head, where everyone could see him. Ida must have loved that. She believed the future depended on young people. Her own son was getting a very early start at being in the middle of things!

• • •

The Barnett family was growing. In November 1897, Ida had her second baby, a son named Herman. A daughter named Ida was born later, in 1901, and Ida gave birth to her last child, Alfreda, in 1904.

Ida had been the oldest child in her family. She had spent a lot of her childhood doing motherly duties. She had cooked, washed, ironed, and cared for her brothers and sisters. By the time Ida got old enough to be a mother herself, she'd had enough! But her feelings changed after she had children of her own. She had happy memories of her parents. They had taught her good values, and she wanted the same kind of family.

For a little while after Herman was born, Ida quit work. That lasted only a few months. Ida couldn't stand to be away from the action. Still, she didn't ignore her family. She visited her children's schools and talked to their teachers. If she left town, she called home to make sure everyone had done their homework.

The children also did many household chores. That was helpful, since Ida hated to keep house. What was the point in dusting? She did it on Monday, and by Tuesday it had to be done again! When she finished drinking her tea, her cup sat empty on the counter all day. Alfreda washed it when she got home from school. Ida didn't like to cook, either (and she wasn't very good at it). Luckily, Ferdinand was a good cook who enjoyed it.

The children knew Ida kept a close eye on them. But they also knew when she was *not* watching. Years later Alfreda remembered how she used to roller-skate inside the house. Her parents were away at work, so they couldn't stop her!

The Barnetts welcomed people into their home. They often invited guests for Sunday dinners and holidays. People who were down on their luck could find somewhere to stay with the Barnetts. One young man who had worked as a cook had later had a bad accident when he'd jumped off a train. He'd gotten hurt and lost his arm. The Barnetts took him in while he recovered. They helped him learn to cook using only one arm.

There were lots of fun times. Ida and Ferdinand got a piano and gave their children music lessons. They played cards together and listened to records. One of Ida's favorite songs was called "The Preacher and the Bear." It was a silly story about a preacher who skipped church one Sunday morning to go hunting, but then ran into an angry grizzly bear. The preacher found himself in a fight for his life!

At the end of the song the preacher begs for help. He says, "Now, Lord, if you can't help me, for goodness' sake don't you help that bear!"[33] Ida couldn't stop laughing whenever they played this song. Maybe that was because she knew what it felt like to be in a battle. Sometimes she was like the preacher. Other times she was more like the grizzly bear. Either way, Ida was always ready for the next fight.

13.
"A BULL IN
A CHINA SHOP"

"Excuse me . . ." Ida tried to get the attention of the saleswoman in the department store.

Ida knew the saleswoman had heard her, but the woman didn't stop to help. She kept walking.

The next clerk would not even look at Ida. She just turned away. Ida knew exactly what was happening. The saleswomen weren't too busy to help her. They had plenty of time to help the white customers. It was only the black ones they ignored.

Well, Ida knew how she could get their attention.

She looked around the store. *There!* She headed over to a display of men's underwear. She picked up a pair and draped them over her arm. She must have looked funny. Proper ladies did not carry around men's underwear in plain sight! Then Ida headed to the door. She acted like she was going to leave the store without paying. The salespeople had no choice now. They had to stop her before she "stole" the underwear!

Ida was tired of facing discrimination all the time. A rude salesclerk in a store was annoying. Still, it was a small thing, and African Americans faced much more serious problems. White employers might not hire them. White landlords might not rent houses to them. Blacks could be beaten or killed for no reason at all. Ida wanted black people to be safe. She wanted them to be treated fairly. When she looked around, she didn't think there was much progress. Nothing happened fast enough!

It's hard for anyone to change things, and Ida had to deal with more obstacles than most people. First of all, she was black. For that reason alone, many white people wouldn't even listen to what she was saying. Plus, she was a woman. At the time, it wasn't common for women to speak their minds. That was especially true in public. Many men believed women should just be quiet. (Many women agreed with them!) Ida thought that was nonsense. She spoke out all the time. She said exactly what was on her mind. She didn't try to insult people, but she also believed in telling the truth. Sometimes she embarrassed people or made them angry. Her short temper also got her into trouble. More than once, she offended someone who could have helped her.

To top it off, she was stubborn. *Very* stubborn. Sometimes that was a good thing. When Ida set herself a task, she did everything she could to make it happen. But she also always wanted to do things her way. She got a reputation as someone who was hard to deal with.

There was one thing African Americans agreed on: they wanted to be treated fairly by white people. But what was fair? They did not always see eye to eye on that. And they did not always agree on how to make their case.

On one side were people like Ida, Frederick Douglass (who had died in 1895), and W. E. B. Du Bois. Du Bois taught history at a college and was also a writer. He became a powerful activist for civil rights. These people believed strongly in black rights. They thought blacks should protest bad treatment from whites. It did no good to keep quiet or back down.

On the other side were people like Booker T. Washington. He was another important leader among blacks. Washington was born a slave in Virginia. After slaves became free, Washington went to school and got an education. He also worked for civil rights.

Washington was less forceful than other black leaders. He didn't want to fight against white people. He wanted to cooperate with them. He thought blacks should agree to go to segregated schools. They should not demand more rights. But whites should give them something in return. They should help blacks go to school and get educated. That would lead to better jobs. Washington hoped that blacks could move up in the world and earn the respect of whites.

At first Ida supported Washington. He was well-known and popular, especially among whites. Ida knew it was important to have support from whites in the fight against racism. But over time she changed her mind about him. She thought Washington didn't stand up enough for African Americans. She believed that he should tell blacks to insist on getting their rights, not just take whatever whites were willing to give them. She also thought he needed to speak out against lynching. But Washington took a very low-key approach. He didn't want to upset his white supporters.

The rocky relationship between Ida and Washington finally fell apart in 1899. It began with the lynching of Sam Hose, a black man from Georgia. Hose had a fight with his boss, a white man named Alfred Cranford. During the argument, Cranford pointed a gun at Hose. Hose was chopping wood at the time. He was scared that Cranford wanted to kill him. To defend himself, Hose threw his ax at Cranford and then ran for his life. Unfortunately, Cranford died from the ax wound, and the people in the town wanted revenge. A mob of thousands got together to lynch Hose. The mob put him through hours of terrible torture and then finally killed him.

It was one of the worst lynchings ever, and when Ida heard about it, she was horrified. Surely, she believed, this event was bad enough that it would convince Booker T. Washington to make a public statement against lynching. At first Washington would not talk about what had happened. More people pressured him to say something, so he finally gave a response. He agreed that mob violence was bad, but he also implied that some lynching victims had committed the crimes they were accused of. Then he said that a lack of education was the problem. He said if more blacks were able to go to school, they wouldn't commit crimes.

Ida was furious with this response. She wrote an article that criticized Washington, but it did not do much good. He had a lot of people on his side. Over the next year, Ida spoke out even more against Washington. She said he did not do enough to help blacks. Instead, he only seemed interested in working on his own projects and making himself look good. Ida did not bother to be polite in her criticism. She was too angry! But Washington did not seem to care what Ida thought. He wrote a letter to his secretary that said, "Miss Wells is fast making herself so ridiculous that everyone is getting tired of her."[34]

Even Ida's old friend T. Thomas Fortune was losing patience with her. In a letter to Washington he called Ida "a bull in a china shop."[35] Maybe Ida's feelings would have been hurt if she had read Fortune's letter. Or maybe she would have thought, *Good!*

That's exactly what I want to be! After all, Ida wasn't trying to tiptoe through a store full of fancy china. She was fighting for the rights of African Americans. Maybe a determined bull was just what the country needed.

14.
WORKING TOGETHER

One day Ida's sons, Herman and Charles, charged up to the doorstep of their house. They panted, breathless from running. Ida went to see what was happening. A gang of white boys stood there. They had chased Herman and Charles all the way home. Maybe the gang wanted to beat them up, but they didn't get the chance. Ida stood in the doorway. All five-feet-four-inches of her stared them down. The white boys turned away. Ida was short, but she was fierce. Plus, she still had that gun she had bought in

Memphis. Everyone in the neighborhood knew that.

The Barnetts had moved to a new street that had mostly white people. It was clear that a black family was not welcome there. When Ida came out onto the porch, her white neighbors went inside and slammed the doors behind them. Now the neighbors' children were harassing her sons.

Ida probably remembered that fight between black and white boys over marbles years before. Her friend Tommie Moss had ended up murdered. Since then, nothing had changed much. It was always white against black, and things were only getting worse.

In 1908 a race riot broke out in Springfield, Illinois. Springfield was about two hundred miles south of where Ida lived. A white woman accused a black man named George Richardson of attacking her. Richardson was arrested and put in jail with another black prisoner. A white mob stormed the jail, wanting to lynch them. The sheriff had expected that, though.

He'd already moved the prisoners to a safe place.

That didn't stop the mob. They wanted blood. When they could not find the two prisoners, they lynched two other black men. Then they robbed and burned the homes and businesses of black people. The governor of Illinois had to send in almost four thousand soldiers to stop the violence. After it was all over, the woman who had accused Richardson came forward. She confessed that she had lied about the whole thing. Richardson went free.

The riot caused at least six deaths. Dozens more people got hurt. The violence shocked everyone— white and black. Somehow the two races had to learn to live together peacefully. If they did not, more people would die. After the riot, community leaders from all over talked about what to do. How could they solve the country's problem of racism? They decided to form a new organization. It would include blacks and whites, and it would have both men and women. They would all work together. Ida traveled to New York to attend a meeting to talk about it. She joined about sixty people to form the new group, which was called the National Association for the Advancement of Colored People (NAACP). It still exists today.

Back home in Chicago, Ida was also looking for ways to stop racism. Shortly after the Springfield riot, she was teaching Sunday school to a group of young adults. They began talking about the riot. Ida was frustrated that many blacks did not seem to care very much about the violence. "What can we do about it?" one man asked.[36] Ida had been trying to answer that question her whole life. Now it was time to help a new generation work on it.

Ida invited her students to meet at her house that afternoon. There they could talk about problems with race and how to improve things. Out of thirty students, three came. It was a small gathering, but it was a start. Ida gave them a challenge. Would each of them come back the next Sunday, and bring a guest?

Over the next few weeks more and more people gathered at Ida's house on Sunday afternoons. They called themselves the Negro **Fellowship** League (NFL). They talked about how to fight racism and the violence that came with it. They also found ways to make the lives of African Americans better. After a couple of years Ida moved the NFL into its own building. Chicago's black citizens could come there to read, play games, and talk about problems they faced. The NFL also helped them find jobs. If a person had nowhere to sleep, he or she could rent a bed for fifteen cents a night. Whatever their problems, Ida tried to help everyone who came through the NFL's door.

One of those people was Annabel Jones. She was twenty-three years old, and she was in trouble. Annabel knew only one life—living with the White family. (The family was white, and their last name was also "White.") Annabel had been a little girl in the South when she went to live with the Whites.

When the family moved, Annabel went with them. Slavery was illegal, but that didn't stop the Whites from treating Annabel like a slave. They beat her and would not allow her to leave the house. They did not pay her for the work she did. Annabel had heard about Ida and the NFL from a black man who sometimes worked for the Whites. Maybe Ida could help Annabel, too.

Ida listened carefully as Annabel told her story. Then she put together a plan. She took Annabel and went to the Whites' house. Ida introduced herself when Mrs. White answered the door. Then Ida went on to tell Mrs. White that she had been keeping Annabel like a slave. This was against the law, and Ida said she had no problem getting Mrs. White in trouble for what she'd done. Mrs. White knew Ida was right. In the end she agreed to pay Annabel for two years of work she had already done. The amount came to more than five hundred dollars. Now Annabel could get on her feet. She had enough money to get a place to live and find a job.

The NFL continued to grow over the next several years, and Ida was very proud of the work they did to help black people.

15.
STANDING UP TO THE SHERIFF

One evening in 1909, Ida tucked Alfreda into bed. Then she sang her five-year-old daughter to sleep. Ida struggled to stay awake herself. Over dinner she and Ferdinand had gone back and forth in a serious discussion. She was worn out. Soon she was fast asleep beside Alfreda.

About an hour later she woke up. Her thirteen-year-old son, Charles, was shaking her shoulder. "Mother, Pa says it is time to go," he said.

"Go where?" Ida asked.

"To take the train to Cairo."[37]

• • •

Charles had been listening to the dinner table conversation a few hours before. Ida and Ferdinand had talked about a lynching in Cairo, Illinois, a town at the southern tip of the state. There, a black man named Will "Frog" James had been accused of murdering a white woman. There was no proof, but he'd been arrested and put in jail anyway. The town's white citizens weren't satisfied with that. They wanted to get their own justice. A few men broke into the jail and took James. Then he was handed over to a mob of ten thousand people. It didn't take long for the crowd to kill him.

Ida had made some progress in her work against lynching. Several states had passed laws banning it. Illinois had another law that took things a step further. It said that if someone was in jail, the police had to protect that person. They could not just sit by and let a lynch mob step in. A sheriff named Frank Davis had been in charge of protecting Frog James. Since Davis had failed, the governor of Illinois had to follow the law and fire him.

But that was not the end of it. Davis had the right to ask for his job back. He just had to show that he had *tried* to protect his prisoner. Davis's **hearing** was coming up in a few days. He had plenty of people lined up to support him, and he would probably win. Then everything would go back to the way it had been.

As the Barnetts ate dinner that night in 1909, Ida and Ferdinand talked about the Davis case. Ferdinand wanted Ida to go to Davis's hearing in Cairo. There she could interview people who knew what had happened. She could argue against the sheriff's getting his job back. Ida resisted. She didn't want to leave home. She thought the people already handling the case should take care of it. Finally Ferdinand let it go. He picked up the newspaper and began to read. He wasn't going to push his wife to travel to Cairo.

At least, that was what Ida thought.

A few hours later, Charles woke her up. Probably Ferdinand had sent him to talk to his mother. When Charles told her it was time to take the train, Ida said, "I told your father downstairs that I was not going."

Charles paused a moment. Then he exclaimed, "Mother, if you don't go, nobody else will!"[38]

Those words were enough for Ida. Her son had reminded her what her duty was. She couldn't leave right then because it was too late in the evening, but she was ready first thing in the morning. Her family went with her to the station and watched her board the train.

Ida had a difficult job in front of her. In Cairo she found out that many of the town's black people supported Sheriff Davis. They believed Frog James had been guilty, and that he'd gotten what he deserved. Ida reminded them that it didn't matter whether James had committed the crime or not. The point was that Sheriff Davis's job had been to protect James. Davis had not done his job. Ida talked to people who admitted that Davis had not even tried to stop the mob. Her report was successful. She convinced the governor not to give Davis his job back.

It was an important victory for Ida. After the Frog James case the governor wrote "Mob violence has no place in Illinois."[39] His words had a big effect. After Frog James, most lynch mobs in the state were stopped in time. Ida's long fight was paying off.

Not long after, Ida stepped in to help another man, named Steve Green. Green had been working for a white man in Arkansas. After his employer had raised his rent, Green had quit and taken another job. That had made his boss angry. He had tracked Green down and shot him. Even though Green had been injured, he'd picked up his own rifle and shot back, killing the man. Green had only been trying to defend himself, but that didn't matter. He was black and the other man was white. Green knew that he was in big trouble. He had fled to Chicago to hide, but the police had found him and arrested him. A sheriff from Arkansas had come to get him and take him back.

When Ida heard about the case, she knew Green was in danger. He would be lynched if he went back to Arkansas. The only hope was to keep him in Illinois. And the way to do *that* was to arrest him again!

Working quickly, Ida got lawyers to look over the paperwork the state of Arkansas had filed to get Green back. There was a mistake—and that gave Ida enough of a reason to step in. She arranged for a judge to approve a legal motion that would stop Green from being taken out of Illinois. The only catch was, they had to reach him in time—and he was already on a train to Arkansas!

Ida knew she had to work fast. She sent messages to every train station along the way. In the messages she stated her offer: a reward of one hundred dollars to anyone who would arrest Green before he left the state.

She was just in time. The train was stopped at the banks of the Mississippi River. As soon as it crossed over, it would be out of Illinois. But before the train started up again, a sheriff boarded the railroad car. He put his hand on Green's shoulder and said, "I arrest this man in the name of the great state of Illinois."[40]

Green went back to Chicago, and Ida kept him hidden as she waited to see what the Arkansas authorities would do next. When she found out they were going to come after Green again, she helped him escape to Canada, where he would be safe. In her autobiography Ida wrote, "He is one Negro who lives to tell the tale that he was not burned alive."[41]

16.
RISING VIOLENCE

When she had been sixteen years old, a train conductor had given Ida a warning. "Don't go to Holly Springs," he'd told her. Ida had gone anyway. She'd had a duty. Now, almost forty years later, another train conductor gave her a similar warning. This time it was, "Don't go to East St. Louis."

Again, Ida didn't follow the conductor's advice. She followed her conscience instead.

• • •

Race problems in the United States were getting worse, even in the North. During World War I (1914–1918), millions of African Americans moved out of the South. They went to Northern cities, where jobs were better. Whites in the North resented them for this. They thought blacks were taking "their" jobs and moving into "their" neighborhoods.

In the summer of 1917 a mob of white men drove through a black neighborhood in East St. Louis, Illinois. They shot at the residents, who fired back. A huge riot broke out and lasted for three days.

Ida wanted to investigate. What exactly had happened? And who would be punished for it? She had a feeling it wouldn't be the city's white population. On July 5, two days after the riot, she traveled by train to East St. Louis. The conductor warned her of the danger in the city. She was a black woman, traveling all by herself. Tensions were high. She had no one to protect her.

Ida insisted. She might have been afraid, but she was more concerned about getting the full story. She got off the train and walked to the city hall, where a man with a gun stood guard. Grimly she asked him how things were. "Bad," he replied.[42]

Ida spent a couple of days in East St. Louis, talking to dozens of people. She determined that about 150 blacks had been killed. Their homes had been set on fire. Thieves had stolen their clothes and other possessions. And just as Ida had suspected, the town's white leaders blamed African Americans.

Just days after the East St. Louis riot, things began heating up in Chester, Pennsylvania. Several black people were attacked throughout the month of July, and by the end of the month a race riot broke out. Less than a month later there was another riot in Houston, Texas. Black citizens there were being harassed, and a rumor started that the police had killed a black soldier. The rumor turned out to be false, but the man's fellow soldiers did not know that. They attacked the police and killed some of them.

They were found guilty and sentenced to death. The men were not given a chance to appeal their sentence. Instead, they were pulled from their jail cells in the middle of the night and hanged.

The year 1918 saw a riot in Philadelphia, Pennsylvania. And by the summer of 1919, racial violence was exploding all over the country. Angry white mobs attacked blacks in South Carolina, Texas, Arizona, Virginia, and Washington, DC. Hundreds died. The period became known as the "red summer" because of all the bloodshed.

Ida feared that Chicago could be next. Blacks and whites there lived together uneasily. It wouldn't take much to set off a riot. The question was, Could she do anything to stop it?

Over the previous few years, more African Americans had moved into the city. They had settled in neighborhoods where mostly white people lived. Many whites became angry. They resented blacks and wanted them out. Things had turned violent when some whites had started setting off bombs at the homes of blacks. One young black girl had been killed. The police had done nothing to prevent these crimes, and they had done nothing to punish the people who'd committed them.

Ida went to the mayor and the police chief. *Please*, she begged them. Please protect blacks from this violence. Please punish the people who commit these crimes. Please step in and treat black people fairly.

They ignored her.

Ida was desperate. In early July 1919, she went to the *Chicago Tribune*. It was one of the city's largest and most powerful newspapers. In an article that she wrote for them, she said that something had to be done "before it is too late."[43]

Again, nothing changed. Just three weeks later Ida's terrible prediction came true. The summer was hot, and many people went to swim in Lake Michigan. There were separate areas for white and black people. In the water some black boys on a raft accidentally floated into the white area. A white man on the beach threw rocks at them and hit one boy in the head. The boy fell into the water and drowned. Chicago's African American community was outraged. The incident set off a race riot that lasted for a week, leaving dozens dead.

Still the killings went on. A couple of months later, in September, about a hundred African American sharecroppers in Arkansas gathered at a church. They worked for white farmers who took most of what they earned. The black farmers wanted better rights and more money, so they held a meeting to talk about what to do. They knew the white farmers would be angry about the meeting, and they knew there might be trouble.

Sure enough, white men came to the meeting to try to break it up. Shots broke out, and one of the white men was killed. That opened the door to more violence. In the next couple of days groups of white men stormed through the town and the farms around it. They killed about a hundred black men, while five white men died in the violence.

Then came the arrests. Not a single white man was arrested, but hundreds of black men were. At the trial twelve men were found guilty and sentenced to death. The jury took less than eight minutes to reach that decision.

Ida was deeply distressed. She hated the violence, but she also hated the unfairness. She could not stop the violence by herself, but maybe she could do something to help.

It had been thirty years since she had left Memphis. Since then, she had not returned to the South— not even once. Even after all this time, Ida knew she was not safe there. If word got out that she was in the South, her life could be in danger.

But there were also twelve men whose lives were on the line.

In early 1920 she boarded a train. It was headed south.

17.
BACK TO
THE SOUTH

A woman named Mrs. Moore walked up to the bars of a jail cell in Little Rock, Arkansas. Inside the cell, her husband and several other men were being kept prisoner. "Boys," Mrs. Moore said loudly, "come and shake hands with my cousin."[44] The prison guard sat in the corner reading the Sunday newspaper. He looked up. He'd seen Mrs. Moore plenty of times before. She came to visit all the time. And that other woman with her? Just another short, elderly, black woman. Nothing seemed out of the ordinary, so he went back to his paper.

There *was* something out of the ordinary, though. That other woman was Ida. At fifty-seven years old, she looked plain and harmless to people who didn't know her. If she kept her head down, no one would bother with her. She did her best to look insignificant as the wives and mothers of the doomed men smuggled her into the prison.

Ida walked up to the cell, and the men shook her hand, just as Mrs. Moore had asked. As they did, Mrs. Moore told them who the woman was—Mrs. Barnett from Chicago. The men's faces lit up. They recognized that name. They knew exactly who Ida was—and it was not Mrs. Moore's cousin!

Shhh. Ida put a finger to her lips to tell the men to stay quiet. She did not want the guard to figure out who she really was. If he did, he would probably throw her out!

Once she had fooled the guard, Ida listened to the prisoners tell their stories. She tried to remember everything they told her. All the time, her mind was racing. How could she help them?

At the end of her visit, the men sang songs for her. Their singing was beautiful, and even the prison **warden** came to listen. The men's voices sounded nice, but Ida did not like the words. The prisoners were singing about how God would welcome them to heaven after they died. When they finished, Ida said, "Dying is the last thing you ought to even think about, much less talk about. Pray to live and believe you are going to get out."[45]

Ida, for one, was going to do everything she could to make that happen. Immediately she began writing up the prisoners' stories. She stayed up all night. She wrote about what they had done—and what they had *not* done. She wrote about how they had been treated unfairly as farmers. She wrote about the abuse they had suffered in prison. Within two days Ida had the makings of a new pamphlet, *The Arkansas Race Riot*. When it was published later that year, it gave a different picture of what had happened.

Meanwhile the NAACP was also working to free the prisoners. Their efforts and Ida's brought a lot of attention to the men's cases, and the courts agreed to listen to appeals. Although it took several years, the guilty **verdicts** were overturned. The men went free.

Some years later, Ida came home to find a young man waiting for her. "Do you know who I am?" he asked. Ida said no. "I am one of them twelve men that you came down to Arkansas about," he told her. After being freed from prison, he had traveled to Chicago. He had wanted to find Ida and thank her for her help. The men had needed her encouragement to not give up. Without that, they might have lost their fight and been executed. Ida's family also met the man while he was there. They must have been proud as he told them, "[We] did as she told us, and now every last one of us is out and enjoying his freedom."[46]

Ida faced a hard time in Chicago after she returned from Arkansas. The city's economy was in bad shape.

The Negro Fellowship League, which Ida had been running for twelve years, was struggling now. Fees at the NFL were very low. It cost only twenty-five cents a month to be a member, and Ida offered services for free to people who could not afford to pay. At first she had found people to donate money to help the NFL stay open. When that was no longer enough, she got a job. She used her own salary to pay the bills. Then she lost her job. Soon she and Ferdinand had gone through all their savings. She could not pay the rent at the NFL building anymore.

One November day in 1920, Ida set out for the NFL offices. When she unlocked the door, her heart sank. In the middle of the night, the landlord had come and cleared it out. The desks, the chairs, and the stove were all gone. Ida knew the NFL was finished. She gathered up the few things that were left and closed the door behind her for the last time.

Tired and discouraged, Ida soon became ill. A week later she went into the hospital. The doctor

18.
STAYING IN THE SPOTLIGHT

The next few years were full of ups and downs. Ida's children were growing up and leaving home. She kept busy by finding new ways to promote civil rights for blacks and women. She joined a new church, where she formed a women's club. She also started a new publication to talk about issues that were important to her. In one important fight she lent her talents to a **labor union** made up of black workers. With her help they got better rights from their company, a powerful railroad.

Lynching was the issue closest to Ida's heart. For

said she had gallstones. That's when balls of hardened fluid collect in a person's gallbladder, one of the body's internal organs. Gallstones can be extremely painful. Ida was very sick and had to have an operation to take them out.

It took her a year to get better. As she stayed home and rested, Ida had a lot of time on her hands. She wondered about how her life was going. She thought hard about the things she had wanted to accomplish. She decided there was still work to do!

thirty years she had fought to stop the terrible practice. The numbers had gone down, but they had not gone down enough. Dozens of African Americans were still being lynched every year. Several states had passed anti-lynching laws, but there was no national law. In 1922 a congressman from Missouri introduced a **bill** that would make the punishment for lynching much worse. If Congress passed the bill, it would become a full law. Ida worked hard for the bill. She was thrilled when the House of Representatives passed it. There was one step left—getting the bill through the Senate. Unfortunately, there were enough senators from the South who did not want the new law. They voted it down. It wasn't until December 2018 that Congress finally passed a law making lynching a crime. It was called the Justice for Victims of Lynching Act of 2018.

In 1930, Ida turned her hand to politics. She entered the election to be one of Illinois's state senators. Ida had almost no money to run a campaign, and she was competing against established people.

She lost in a landslide. But a few years before, it would have been out of the question for her to even run. African Americans—and women—were taking steps forward.

Ida was old enough to know that life brought both wins and losses. The key was to always keep trying. Ida did not let herself get discouraged by the loss. She had plenty of other projects to keep her busy. One of them was to tell the story of her own life.

The lamp on Ida's table burned brightly into the night. Papers were spread out all around her. Extra leaves had been put into the table to make it bigger. Ida needed as much room as she could get!

Alfreda watched as her mother's pen scratched furiously across the page. Sometimes Ida used a new sheet of paper. Other times she grabbed a letter someone had sent her and scribbled on the back. She didn't care—she used whatever was handy. She had an important story to tell. This time it was her own.

Ida had begun writing her autobiography after a young black woman had come to her with a question. The woman had gone to a meeting where the leader had asked each woman to name her hero. That was an easy question. "Ida B. Wells-Barnett," the young woman had answered. But she had not been ready for the next question. The leader asked *why* Ida was the young woman's hero. The young woman had not really known. She'd been determined to find out more.

Soon after that Ida had gotten a visitor. "Mrs. Barnett, I couldn't tell why I thought [you were my hero]," the young woman had confessed. "I have heard you mentioned so often by that name, so I gave it. I was dreadfully embarrassed. Won't you please tell me what it was you did, so the next time I am asked such a question I can give an intelligent answer?"[47]

Ida found out that the girl was only twenty-five years old. No wonder she didn't know much about Ida's work. Most of the things Ida had done had happened before the girl was even born. Ida thought it was important for young people to understand their history. She could help by writing about her own experiences.

Ida had spent her whole life fighting racism. In her book she remembered all these battles. She also wrote about her childhood and other personal events. It was a good thing that she had decided to write everything down. A fire at her house burned many of her other papers. Today, her autobiography is one of the few things that is left to remember her by.

Unfortunately, Ida did not finish her manuscript. For some reason she put down her pen in the middle of a sentence and went to do something else. She never returned to her book. One Saturday in March 1931, Ida went out shopping. When she got home, she did not feel well. She was tired and went to bed. She didn't get up for church the next morning. By Monday, Ferdinand was worried. He and Alfreda took her to the hospital. By then Ida was very sick. A few days later she died. Her kidneys had failed. She was sixty-eight years old.

The funeral was what Ida had wanted. There was no shouting. People did not cry loudly or wave their arms around in grief. Instead there were just "plain, earnest, sincere words" from her friends and family. The minister noted simply, "She will be missed."[48]

As a final good-bye a singer sang the hymn "I've Done My Work."

Indeed, she had.

Epilogue
"THE LIGHT OF TRUTH"

After her death much of Ida's life was forgotten. Her name did not appear often in history books. The details of her work were buried in dusty, old newspapers and boxes of private letters and papers.

But everywhere there was progress for African Americans. By the 1950s the civil rights movement was in full swing. Its goal was to get equal rights for all Americans. In 1954 the US Supreme Court ruled that segregated schools were illegal. A year later, in 1955, a black woman named Rosa Parks refused to give up her bus seat for a white person. More and more, blacks were demanding their rights. They went to hotels and restaurants even when there were signs that said WHITES ONLY. They held meetings and marched together. Slowly things were changing.

In 1964, President Lyndon B. Johnson signed the Civil Rights Act. This law protected Americans from discrimination. Among other things, it made it illegal to treat black Americans unfairly just because of their color.

Ida would have loved to see that day! And she would have loved that her children *did* live to see it. So did millions of other black children. In her autobiography Ida had written that she was telling her story for young African Americans. She wanted them to know their history, and she wanted them to fight for their future. For many years, though, her book just sat in a drawer. Then, in 1970, her daughter Alfreda got it published. It was called *Crusade for Justice*. That was a perfect way to describe Ida's life.

Ida won some of her battles and lost others. But she was a brave woman who did not back down. She did not ask for praise, and she did not let setbacks discourage her for long. She just did what had to be done. "The way to right wrongs is to turn the light of truth upon them," Ida once said.[49] That was how she chose to help people. She told the truth—one article, one speech, one protest at a time.

Most of all, she never gave up. She worked until the very end of her life. After she died, a new generation of people picked up the fight. Through them, Ida is still helping to make a difference.

Glossary

activist someone who works for a cause or an issue

appeal to argue that a legal decision was wrong and to ask a higher court to listen to the case

autobiography a book written by someone about himself or herself

barge a large, flat boat used to carry freight

bill a proposal for a new law

boycott the act of not buying or using something as a way to protest

civil rights legal rights that all citizens have to make sure they are treated equally

condemn to say that something is thoroughly wrong

discrimination unfair treatment of people because of their race, gender, religion, or other personal characteristic

GLOSSARY

epidemic an outbreak of a disease that affects a lot of people all at once

escort to go with someone, to accompany

fellowship a sense of community or companionship, especially with other people with similar interests

hearing a time for people to give information in a legal case, before a full trial

interracial involving two or more different races

journalist a person who gathers and reports news, such as a writer for a newspaper

labor union a group of workers who join together so that they have more power to fight for changes such as better conditions and pay

lawsuit a case that comes before a legal court to be settled

lyceum a club whose members have lectures, concerts, and similar activities

lynching the killing of a person by a mob, often in a cruel way, without having the legal right to do so

podium a platform that someone stands on when making a speech to an audience

GLOSSARY

prejudice a negative opinion of someone, without a good reason

press journalists and news media such as newspapers, radio, and television, taken as a group

racism the belief that one race of people is better than another

riot a violent fight or disturbance involving a large number of people

rumpus an uproar, or trouble that gets a lot of attention

segregated separated by race

seize to take hold of, grab

sharecropper a farmer who works on someone else's land in return for a share of the earnings

streetcar a vehicle that runs on rails on city streets

subscribe to pay money to receive something for a set period of time, such as a newspaper

suppress to prevent something from happening or being found out

verdict the final decision in a trial, such as "guilty" or "not guilty"

warden the person in charge of a prison

Endnotes

1   Ida B. Wells, *Crusade for Justice: The Autobiography of Ida B. Wells*, ed. Alfreda M. Duster (Chicago: University of Chicago Press, 1970), 12.

2   Wells, *Crusade*, 9.

3   Wells, *Crusade*, 11.

4   Wells, *Crusade*, 16.

5   Ida B. Wells, *The Memphis Diary of Ida B. Wells*, ed. Miriam DeCosta-Willis (Boston: Beacon Press, 1995), 141.

6   Wells, *Diary*, 23.

7   Wells, *Diary*, 56.

8   Wells, *Diary*, 138.

9   "The Widow Bud," performed by A. S. Johnson, recorded at Yuba City FSA Camp, August 18, 1940, Library of Congress, digital audio, 4:02, https://www.loc.gov/item/toddbib000203/.

10 Wells, *Diary*, 102.

11 Linda O. McMurry, *To Keep the Waters Troubled: The Life of Ida B. Wells* (New York: Oxford University Press, 1998), 111.

12 Wells, *Crusade*, 32.

13 Wells, *Crusade*, 39.

14 Wells, *Crusade*, 42.

15 Wells, *Crusade*, 51.

ENDNOTES

16   Wells, *Crusade*, 54.

17   Wells, *Crusade*, 55.

18   Wells, *Crusade*, 64.

19   Wells, *Crusade*, 62.

20   Wells, *Crusade*, 61.

21   Wells, *Crusade*, 61.

22   Wells, *Crusade*, 79.

23   Ida B. Wells-Barnett, *Selected Works of Ida B. Wells-Barnett*, comp. Trudier Harris (New York: Oxford University Press, 1991), 16.

24   Paula J. Giddings, *Ida: A Sword Among Lions* (New York: Amistad, 2008), 250.

25   Wells, *Crusade*, 73.

26   Wells, *Crusade*, 86.

27   Wells, *Crusade*, 86.

28   Wells, *Crusade*, 87–88.

29   Mia Bay, *To Tell the Truth Freely: The Life of Ida B. Wells* (New York: Hill and Wang, 2009), 190.

30   Giddings, 349.

31   Giddings, 305.

32   Wells-Barnett, *Selected Works*, 146.

33   Joe Arzonia, "The Preacher and the Bear" (Philadelphia: The Morris Music Pub. Co., 1904), https://digitalcommons.library .umaine.edu/mmb-vp/1395.

34   Bay, 246.

35   Bay, 244.

36   Wells, *Crusade*, 299.

37   Wells, *Crusade*, 311.

38   Wells, *Crusade*, 311.

39   Bay, 280.

ENDNOTES

40   Wells, *Crusade*, 336.

41   Wells, *Crusade*, 337.

42   Wells, *Crusade*, 384.

43   Kristina DuRocher, *Ida B. Wells: Social Reformer and Activist* (New York: Routledge, 2017), 134.

44   Wells, *Crusade*, 401.

45   Wells, *Crusade*, 403.

46   Wells, *Crusade*, 404.

47   Wells, *Crusade*, 3.

48   McMurry, 337.

49   DuRocher, 1.

Bibliography

Bay, Mia. *To Tell the Truth Freely: The Life of Ida B. Wells*. New York: Hill and Wang (Farrar, Straus & Giroux), 2009.

Davidson, James West. *"They Say": Ida B. Wells and the Reconstruction of Race*. New York: Oxford University Press, 2007.

DuRocher, Kristina. *Ida B. Wells: Social Reformer and Activist*. New York: Routledge, 2017.

Giddings, Paula J. *Ida: A Sword Among Lions*. New York: Amistad / HarperCollins, 2008.

Guide to the Ida B. Wells Papers, 1884–1976. University of Chicago Library, 2009. https://www.lib.uchicago.edu/e/scrc/findingaids /view.php?eadid=ICU.SPCL.IBWELLS#idp85062864.

Harlan, Louis R., and Raymond W. Smock, eds. *The Booker T. Washington Papers, Volume 5: 1899–1900*. Urbana, Illinois: University of Chicago Press, 1976.

McMurry, Linda O. *To Keep the Waters Troubled: The Life of Ida B. Wells*. New York: Oxford University Press, 1998.

BIBLIOGRAPHY

Schechter, Patricia A. *Ida B. Wells-Barnett and American Reform, 1880–1930.* Chapel Hill: University of North Carolina Press, 2001.

Silkey, Sarah L. *Black Woman Reformer: Ida B. Wells, Lynching, and Transatlantic Activism.* Athens: University of Georgia Press, 2015.

Thompson, Mildred I. *Ida B. Wells-Barnett: An Exploratory Study of an American Black Woman, 1893–1930.* Brooklyn, New York: Carlson Publishing, 1990.

Wells, Ida B. *Crusade for Justice: The Autobiography of Ida B. Wells.* Edited by Alfreda M. Duster. Chicago: University of Chicago Press, 1970.

Wells, Ida B. *The Light of Truth: Writings of an Anti-Lynching Crusader.* Edited by Mia Bay. New York: Penguin Books, 2014.

Wells, Ida B. *The Memphis Diary of Ida B. Wells.* Edited by Miriam DeCosta-Willis. Boston: Beacon Press, 1995.

Wells-Barnett, Ida B. *Selected Works of Ida B. Wells-Barnett.* Compiled by Trudier Harris. New York: Oxford University Press, 1991.

About the Author

DIANE BAILEY has written dozens of books for kids and teens, on everything from sports to science, but her very favorite topics are on history and the people who made it. She also helps other authors by editing their books. When she's not working, she likes to take walks (really fast—try to keep up!), plant flowers (and hope they don't die), and watch scary movies (as long as they come out okay at the end). Diane has two grown sons and lives in Lawrence, Kansas.